More people play football than any other game.
Millions more watch it.

TV cameras film football matches so millions of people can watch the same match all over the world.

Manchester United winning the 1996 FA Cup Final.
The FA Cup is one of the world's most famous football competitions.

Youth football

Top professional clubs have youth teams for boys who show great skill at football.

Liverpool youth football team

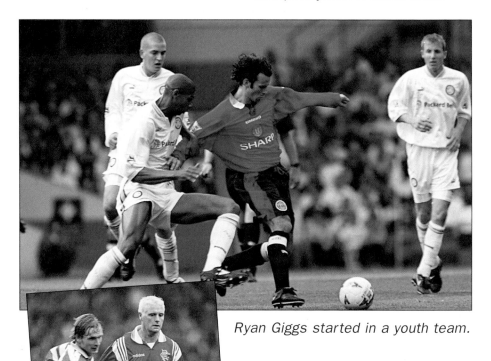

Ryan Giggs started in a youth team.

Paul Gascoigne also started in a youth team.

4

796.334

The world's favourite game

Football is the world's most popular game. The top teams are seen all over the world.

Brazil beat Italy in the 1994 World Cup Final. They have won the World Cup four times.

It is popular because it is a fast game and it does not have a lot of difficult rules. It is a good game for young players because it is fairly safe.

Also, it doesn't cost much. You only need a ball to play.

Two boys playing football in Rio de Janeiro, Brazil

Manchester United played Liverpool in the 1996 FA
Cup Final. Both sides had players who had started in
the youth sides.

*Steve McManaman,
Dominic Matteo and
Robbie Fowler
all started in
youth teams.*

There is also an FA competition for players from school
and county teams.

Bedford Town won the Senior Cup County Championship in 1996.

Bedford Citizen and Times

Many colleges in North America have teams. Americans call the game soccer.

Soccer is the most popular college game for women in North America.

Europe has a competition for boys under 16.

The 1996 European Under-16 final was played in France.

Top professional players start early in Europe.
The big clubs take six-year-old boys into youth teams.

Amsterdam's Ajax is the most famous side in Holland. Dennis Bergkamp was an Ajax youth player. He went into the first team when he was 16. He played for Holland at 18.

Dennis Bergkamp played for Ajax in 1990 and for Arsenal in 1996.

Football stars

Football is a team game, but it has star players in key positions.

STAR DEFENDER

Paolo Maldini of Italy is one of the world's great defenders. He tackles strongly to defend his team's goal.

STAR FORWARD

The forward is also called the striker. His job is to score goals. The big clubs pay huge fees to buy their strikers.

Alan Shearer is a striker for England and Newcastle. In 1996 Newcastle paid £15 million for him. This was the biggest fee ever.

STAR MID-FIELDER

The mid-fielder has to be an all-round player. He must be able to pass, run fast to attack and score too.

Juninho playing mid-field for his country, Brazil

STAR GOALKEEPER

A great goalkeeper can make a difficult save look easy.

Peter Schmeichel playing in goal for Denmark

Players of the future

The Tottenham Hotspurs scout saw James Evans play when he was ten. James trained with Spurs until he was 15. He trained once a week after school.

At 15 James played for Spurs youth side at weekends. He was picked to join Spurs when he was 16. He left school and joined the youth team. He'll play with the team for two years.

James's week

Monday

James does his college work with the other boys.

Their teacher comes to Spurs to teach them.

He spends from 11.00 am to 2.00 pm every day in the classroom. Then it takes James two hours to get home.

Tuesday

This is the first day of proper training.

James does fitness work and running.

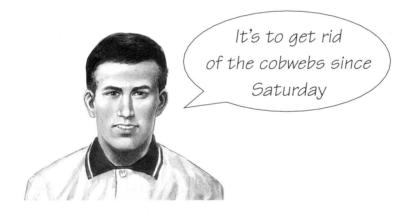

It's to get rid of the cobwebs since Saturday

Wednesday

The two youth teams play five-a-side games.

There are 22 boys aged from 16–18 in the Spurs youth teams.

Thursday

James works on his ball skills.

He practises shooting, passing and dribbling.

We do 'back four' practice too

The 'back four' are the team's defenders.

Friday

Friday's an easy day

The team gets ready for its game on Saturday.

The coach helps the team plan their match tactics.

Saturday

James and the team kick off their game at 11.00 am.

After their own match they will watch the Spurs first team if they have a home game.

All the boys in the youth team get free tickets to the matches.

What's the best thing about being in the youth team?

"It's the games, and the fun," James says.

What's the worst thing?

"The jobs!" says James. "We have to clean the first team's boots, and sort out all the dirty kit."

What's James's ambition?

"That's easy. It's to get in the first team!"

Is football a girl's game, too?

Yes! Women and girls all over the world play football. Over a million women and girls in the United States play football. The US women's team won the 1996 Olympic competition.

The first Women's World Cup was won by the US in 1991.

In Norway just as many women play football as men.
Some of the best British women players go to play in
teams in Italy, Sweden and Germany.

Women's football is the fastest-growing sport in Britain. Over 15,000 women play. There are no professional teams yet.

There is an FA Women's Cup in April every year. There is also a Women's Premier League. Women's teams at Arsenal and Liverpool play in the club kits.

Girls aged from 11–16 can play in junior teams.

In 1996 there was a Festival of Football for girls.

Girls played games and had free coaching.

Football skills

KEY TIPS

ALWAYS
Keep your eye on the ball.
Plan your pass.

PASSING

Want to kick dead ahead? Use an:

Instep pass

- knee over ball
- heel up
- toe down
- kick ball with your instep

ball goes forward

Want to kick to the side? Use a:

Side foot pass

- turn leg out
- kick ball with the inside of your foot

ball will go this way

Want to get round a defender? Use a:

Swerving pass

- kick the right side of the ball with the outside of your left foot
- ball will swerve left
- kick the left side of the ball with the outside of your right foot
- ball will swerve right

ball will swerve right

Want to get over a defender? Use a:

Lofted pass

- swing kicking leg back
- keep your knee behind the ball

kick ball here

HEADING

Forward header

- keep your eye on the ball
- lean back to get power
- move your head to meet the ball
- hit the ball with your forehead

Sideward header

- hit the ball with the top of your forehead
- as you hit, turn your head to where you want the ball to go

Backward header

- lean forward to get power
- hit the ball with the top of your head

TACKLING

If you have time, use a:

Blocking tackle

- move in to tackle soon
- face the other player
- kick the ball just as the other player goes to pass

To clear the ball fast, use a:

Sliding tackle

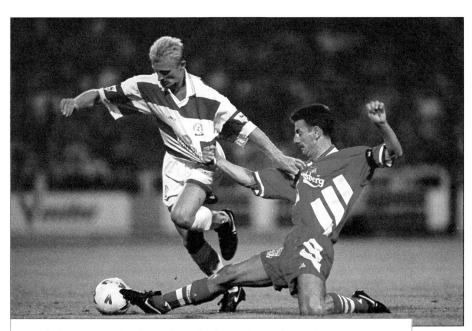

- slide across in front just before the other player passes
- don't trip them up or they will get a free kick

DRIBBLING

Fooling the other player

- look ahead, but keep the ball in view
- don't kick the ball too far forward
- speed up suddenly
- lean one way and then go the other

SHOOTING

- shoot low and kick the top half of the ball
- aim at the post furthest from the goalkeeper
- shoot fast and don't wait for a clear view of the goal
- follow through with your kicking foot

GOAL-KEEPING

The leaping save

- keep your eye on the ball
- face the ball
- hands behind the ball

Save with your body

- use your body to block the ball
- curl your arms round the ball

The diving save

- move on your toes first
- push off with the foot near the ball
- don't land on your front
- relax as you hit the ground to keep hold of the ball

The kit

All football kit is made of
light materials. The ball has
to stay dry in the rain. If it
soaked up water, it would get
too heavy to play with.

The shirt and shorts dry fast.
The material won't pull out
of shape.

The boots have to be light too.

This style of boot has extra strips of leather on the instep. These strips help to send the ball further

The club strip is now a fashion item. The club's fans buy the strip to wear themselves. This earns the clubs millions of pounds.

A club uses designers when it wants a new strip.

The designers will draw three or four different designs. Each design is made up into shirt and shorts. The club chooses the one it wants.

The World Cup

The World Cup is the most famous international competition. It is held in a different country every four years. It began in South America in 1930.

The English took football to South America in the last century. South Americans loved the game. South American teams have won 8 out of the 15 World Cups.

ARE SHOOT-OUTS FAIR?

The 1994 final was a draw.
Brazil won after a penalty shoot-out.
Many people think this is not fair.
The next World Cup may change this
way of deciding draws.

THE "HAND OF GOD" GOAL

In 1986 Argentina beat England 2–1 in the quarter finals. The Argentinian Captain Diego Maradona scored the winning goal. Film replays showed that this goal was a handball. Maradona said the goal was scored "By the Hand of God."

How much do you know about

1 What do Americans call football?

2 Which nation had produced most World Cup winning teams by 1994?

3 Which youth team did Dennis Bergkamp play for?

4 Which National team does Junhino play for?

5 When was the first Women's World Cup?

6 When is the FA Women's Cup held?

7 Name three different types of pass.

Football?

8 When you do a sliding tackle,

do you kick the ball:

a) just before the other player passes?

b) at the same time as the other player?

c) just after they've kicked it?

9 What position is Paolo

Maldini most famous for playing?

10 What was the biggest fee ever

paid for a UK player before 1997?

11 Who scored the goal

"By the Hand of God" in

the 1986 World cup Final?

12 How often is the World Cup held?

Answers are on the inside back cover

Index